B

2/95

FLYING SQUIRRELS

NIGHTTIME ANIMALS

Lynn M. Stone

The Rourke Corporation, Inc.
Vero Beach, Florida 32964

Edited by Sandra A. Robinson

PHOTO CREDITS
All photos © Maslowski Photo

Library of Congress Cataloging-in-Publication Data

Stone, Lynn M.
    Flying squirrels / by Lynn M. Stone.
        p. cm. — (Nighttime animals)
    Includes index.
    Summary: Discusses the physical characteristics, habitats, and
behavior of flying squirrels and describes the different kinds.
    ISBN 0-86593-298-0
    1. Flying squirrels—Juvenile literature. [1. Flying squirrels.
2. Squirrels.] I. Title. II. Series: Stone, Lynn M. Nighttime animals.
QL737.R68S74   1993
599.32'32—dc20   93-4146
                                                CIP
                                                 AC

Printed in the USA

TABLE OF CONTENTS

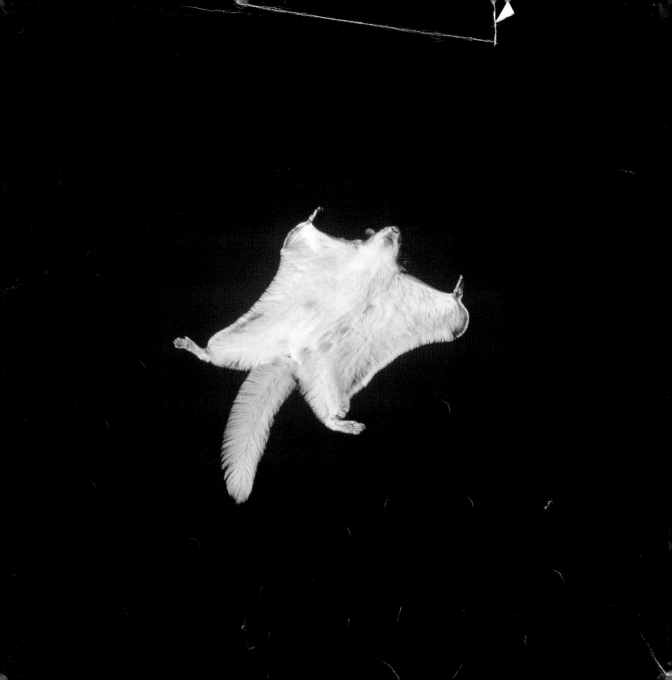

FLYING SQUIRRELS

Flying squirrels don't have wings, so they can't really fly. They do, however, leap into space and glide from one tree to another with great skill.

The ability to glide several feet through the air separates the little flying squirrels from other tree squirrels. Flying squirrels are different in another way, too. They are highly **nocturnal**—active at night. Flying squirrels move at night through the trees that gray and fox squirrels use in daylight.

Flying squirrels flatten their lightweight bodies and glide like flying carpets of fur

HOW FLYING SQUIRRELS LOOK

Flying squirrels are usually a shade of brown or gray. They are smaller and flatter than other tree squirrels. They have bigger eyes, too, which help them see in dim light.

Flying squirrels have slender bodies so that they can glide. They also have a fold of loose skin along both sides of their bodies. The skin, called a gliding **membrane,** folds up when the squirrel isn't gliding.

Moonlight and the flying squirrel's big eyes help it measure glide distances and find food

NATURE'S GLIDER

A flying squirrel can climb and it can walk, but it does most of its traveling by gliding. As a flying squirrel pushes off into space, it spreads its four legs. The loose gliding membrane along its sides stretches open tightly, like an umbrella.

The squirrel can make sharp turns and control its magic carpet ride by tightening or loosening its membrane and raising its tail.

The glide always takes the squirrel from a higher perch to a lower perch.

With its gliding membrane stretched open, a flying squirrel launches itself from a tree

KINDS OF FLYING SQUIRRELS

Flying squirrels of many **species,** or kinds, live in Asia, Europe, Africa and North America. Two species of flying squirrels that are nearly alike—the northern and southern flying squirrels—live in the United States and Canada.

Both kinds have soft, thick fur. Northern flying squirrels are a little larger. Neither species, however, has a head and body length of more than 14 inches. Flying squirrels weigh just 2 to 8 ounces.

This southern flying squirrel weighs only about 4 ounces

Nighttime visitors, flying squirrels raid a bird feeder

A flying squirrel, tail up to slow its glide, braces for a landing

WHERE FLYING SQUIRRELS LIVE

Flying squirrels live as far north as trees grow in Canada and Alaska, and south to Texas and Florida.

A flying squirrel's tree home is usually a hole once used by a woodpecker. Sometimes flying squirrels build summer nests of sticks in a tree. They also nest in bird boxes and in attics.

A flying squirrel pokes its head from a woodpecker's former home

WHAT FLYING SQUIRRELS EAT

Flying squirrels eat many foods, including nuts, seeds, fruits, berries, birds' eggs, moths and other insects.

Once in a while flying squirrels nibble on meat scraps. Flying squirrels have been caught in traps for other animals that were baited with meat.

Because they are active at night, flying squirrels usually escape daylight **predators** such as hawks. Even so, they are hunted at night by bobcats, raccoons, weasels and owls.

A flying squirrel dines on a night flyer, the cecropia moth

FLYING SQUIRREL HABITS

When day fades into night at dusk, flying squirrels leave their nests to look for food. They hunt alone, but flying squirrels can be quite **social.** Several of them may share a winter nest.

Winter doesn't end the flying squirrels' work, but it does slow them down. Windy and wet weather can also keep flying squirrels "indoors."

*A flying squirrel leaves its home—
a bird box—as night falls*

BABY FLYING SQUIRRELS

A female flying squirrel usually has two **litters** each year. Most litters have two babies, although a flying squirrel may have as many as six.

A baby flying squirrel's eyes stay closed for about a month. By the time it is two months old, the baby squirrel no longer depends on its mother's milk. It eats solid foods.

Young flying squirrels grow up in less than a year. Flying squirrels in captivity have lived up to 13 years.

A mother flying squirrel gently carries her baby in her mouth

FLYING SQUIRRELS AND PEOPLE

Flying squirrels are plentiful in many places, but most people never see them. Like other nocturnal animals, flying squirrels hide during the day, which is when people would be likely to spot them.

People are a threat to flying squirrels when they destroy the squirrels' **habitats,** the woodlands where they live. Two kinds of southern flying squirrels in North Carolina, Tennessee, Virginia and West Virginia are **endangered**—in danger of disappearing forever. Their biggest problem is the destruction of their woodland homes.

Glossary

endangered (en DANE jerd) — in danger of no longer existing; very rare

habitat (HAB uh tat) — the kind of place in which an animal lives, such as woodland

litter (LIH ter) — a group of babies born together of the same mother

membrane (MEM brain) — thin, stretchable skin often in the form of a pouch or flap

nocturnal (nahk TUR nul) — active at night

predator (PRED uh tor) — an animal that kills other animals for food

social (SO shul) — spending considerable time in the company of others of the same kind

species (SPEE sheez) — within a group of closely-related living things, one certain kind or type (*southern* flying squirrel)

INDEX